THE
ANSWER
LIES
WITHIN

THE
ANSWER
LIES
WITHIN

VEDIC WISDOM *Demystified*

NEW EXPANDED EDITION

RACHNA CHOPRA

"Thank you for this inspirational book. The words of prayer are very powerful, and I say them everyday. I find that I have reached a place of great peace." —INGRID LORENZ, Australia

"Delighted to read about the power of inner speech to achieve success. I am a professional Psychologist, using a number of techniques to bring about change. However, your techniques are convincing, and have potential because they are rooted in the science of Vedic spirituality." —ANIRUDH PANDEY, India

"Your words are simply superb, to say the least. Each time I read them, they give me a new enthusiasm and an inner power to WIN." —ANASTASIA WELLS, USA

"Your writings gave me back my sense of self-respect, belief in basic human values, and the confidence to build myself back up." —SARASWATI RUIZ, USA

"Soul stirring book. I began nurturing plants and establishing a rapport with them, and experienced a rare two way exchange. No egoism, no hatred, no jealousy. Only love, love and love." —SOLVEIG THOMAS, Germany

"This is my Bible." —AMIT, Amazon buyer

The words filled in the following pages
have emerged from the stirrings of the heart,
and promptings of the spirit.

CONTENTS

PART 2: MEDITATIONS

FOREWORD

The Answer Lies Within is a collection of published essays by the author, with a common theme of personal empowerment, accountability, and dedicated effort towards the goal of self-realization. These essays demystify Eastern wisdom and deity worship, and clarify the fundamentals of yoga, breath work and meditative practices.

The first edition of this book was an exclusive collection of inspirational column *Bridge of Light*, published in the *Hindustan Times*, a leading national daily of India, in 2001. These writings (amongst first penning by the author) poured forth effortlessly, as though a bridge of light was indeed channeling higher inspiration. The column soon became popular across all ages, cultures and religions, and got published in book form in 2002.

This expanded edition preserves the original writings, and incorporates other columns by the author published in the *Pioneer* (2002), *Daily News and Analysis* (2005), and *Kosmic Life* (2008).

The first part of the book comprises of reflections on the Self, while the second part contains practices and meditations towards realizing it. The division is arbitrary, of course, as reflections can be meditations and vice-a-versa. All that is asked of you, is that you take a momentary break from intellectualism, and put your heart to work!

Have you ever pondered why were you born, or were you?

Your breath is taken to be proof of your existence. Your heartbeat confirms that you are still alive. Tears on your eyelash tell that you are still suffering. Yet, will you cease to be when the heart stops its beat? Will you die when the breath swells and disperses? Will you be no more when your body turns cold and lifeless?

You are led from one situation to the next, from one place to another, from one thought to the second. This chaos almost seems deliberate, intended to make you lose your identity, your address. Whose intention was it?

Nobody you know can tell.

You roll in dreams and desires. You possess, knowing well that one note of destiny can snatch it all away. You smile, with the sword of sadness hung over your head. There is light, then shade. Everything appears real, then false, then real and false again. Who will free you from this twin bondage of rest and unrest?

You work, love, pray. Yet there is an emptiness that is not filled. A void threatens to overpower. Can you be fearless? Can you be free?

When you speak you exist. When you become silent, everything does! Where do you disappear when you sleep, which is that world and which is this? Who decides the moment of sunrise and sunset? If there is a meaning to existence, what needs to be realized? Did you happen to creation or did life happen to you? Will life give you that one chance or will you miss? Can you choose the hour of death. Or rather, must you die?

If you do not ask these questions, you are lucky. If you question, and not fervently find the answer, you remain a fool. If you question, and seek the answer from the outside, you haven't understood. When you question, wait for no one to reply, do not believe if someone does—you are on the right track. The final piece of the puzzle lies in our own recesses. The answer lies within, in the domain of the questionless.

Part One

REFLECTIONS

1.

CHERISH LIFE BY DARING TO DREAM

Think of it. Between one day and the next, our entire life gets spent. Oft between fifty summers and fifty rains, our season comes to a conclusion, our dreams come to an abrupt halt. Our attachments stare awkwardly, not knowing where to tiptoe next. God keeps the perfumed eternity all for himself, while we spin on the wheel of *saṃsāra* (cyclic existence). To wish to live forever may seem foolish, yet if God extended his hand of immortality, we would hold it forever. Perhaps the ideal of deathlessness and unbroken life is just a culmination of our wishful thinking. Yet if this world is but a nest of dreams, let us courage to conceive of a flower that never withers, and a raindrop that never dries! Let us claim a share in our timeless inheritance and create our highest miracle, by exploring any and every tool on the way—reflections, meditations, visualizations, affirmations, yoga or plain simple dreaming, that will lead us to our goal. There is no denying that we are linked to our divine origin through a never-to-be-severed umbilical cord, a bridge of light. Times when we receive supernatural strength after a simple heartfelt prayer, confirm its presence. Let us strengthen this link till we finally blend in infinity. What do we have to lose after all, except our fears.

There are no boundaries,
except the ones we create.

2.

MAKE VULNERABILITY YOUR STRENGTH

At times, life's meaning eludes us. At other times, we give up finding it. Doubts, confusions and personal hardships drift us into a mechanical existence. Switching from 'why we live' enquiry to 'we live' acceptance, we hush our search for meaning in a corner. Yet, it lurks hideously still, waiting to pounce on us during times when we have to meet life in the eye, and understand our equation with it. It is not easy to live without myths, survive without beliefs, or acknowledge our insignificance in the scheme of things. It is difficult to accept our helplessness, and complete ignorance about who we are, why are we here, and how shall we live. We ponder, but our intelligence does not lead us anywhere, for we have embarked on territories where reason does not grow. We move in all directions, not knowing what is true or for real, like a child groping in the dark. Till such time that you gain a clue, cherish this very vulnerability that you mostly do not allow yourself to recognize. This *not knowing* is our anchor to reach the divine threshold. Keep questioning. Do not give up on finding the truth, for self-effort is our dharma. But after you have explored and exhausted your powers and possibilities, invoke strength and surrender the limitations of your understanding to faith. Allow the ocean to drift you to the shore.

Sacrifice reason to love.
Be led in knowing you do not know.

3.

THERE IS ONLY ONE CHANCE—NOW

The most unholy act that we can indulge in, is to be in the next moment. It is indeed the greatest of sins, the king of ignorance, and the saddest crime we can possibly commit against ourselves. The instant we move to the future, we die, because in the chain of events to come, ultimately death is next. When we fix our gaze on a salvation that lies in the morrow, we turn a blind eye and a deaf ear to the pulsating throbbing life at hand, and forego the freedom we can access right now. If we are able to appreciate the present moment, are wholly interested in what is here, visible and real, we need no stringent practices, rituals or austerities. Being in the present itself is an enormous practice. It demands courage to be able to drop the load of the past, and constant seamless awareness to not enter the future. It requires vigilance, to not permit even a single thought to escape without your observing it. The person who can live in the now, is indeed the one to be worshipped. Chop off your connection to what would be, or has been. Shed your conception of future, if it clouds your attention to the present. Be faithful to the hour at hand. As you live each moment *for* the moment, the deliverance that you seek will find you.

The present moment has infinite possibility.

4.

THE ANSWER LIES WITHIN

There comes a time when we come to terms with the hard fact, that there is nobody outside of us. We have only ourselves for better or for worse, and no miracles would possibly rush to our rescue. When we accept the plain ordinary human that we are, nothing more *but* nothing less, suddenly a beautiful event occurs. We gain the obvious power to do what is in our capacity to the hilt, and begin to trust ourselves as our savior. This is a power we never exploited before, as our eyes were always set on the luster of sages or gurus that we idolize. Awe of other men and their wisdom never permitted us to communicate with our own light. We have become habituated to taking our freedom from another, and treating our inborn bliss as another's gift! Slowly, as we begin to insist on ourselves, a thousand miracles unfold. Our (very human) capabilities acquire a divine dimension, and stretch infinitely. We become our own power source, and no longer dismiss our wisdom because it is our own. We start to command our fate, solve our riddles and enrich our circumstance. At this junction, the great paradox resurfaces. You shiver to ponder the possibility, that during all this time of strife and struggle, and your long quest for union, you and your Shiva were already one!

You are the secret code you must unravel.

5.

ESSENCE OF YOGA

Yoga is the means of acquiring stillness of mind, and steadiness of purpose. You need not practice many postures. Just pick one, and master it. If you get bored with one, pick a few that suit your temperament. Master them. It is the discipline that yields the fruit, not so much the posture. Watch how long can you retain a single posture, any posture, without moving or glancing sideways. Just sit cross-legged with a straight spine, and stare into blank space, at the tip of your nose, on the third eye in between the eyebrows, or on a candle. This *just sitting* is an important first step. In traditional terms, this is referred to as *kaya sthairyam*, or steadying of the physical body, that in turn steadies the mind. Yet it is not the object of attention that matters as much, but attention itself. Thankfully, we do have a choice as to where we direct our attention. Attention power is always in our hands. We can use it for anything we wish to manifest, such as success at work, joy in a relationship, or achievement of an ambition. Yet, the true purport of yoga is to collect attention for realization of our unity with the indivisible cosmic principle. This is the highest goal. Like a bath is for cleansing of the body, yoga is for the purification of the soul. The means of acquiring unwavering attention is practice, just like with anything else.

As big fish eats small fish, let higher objectives override small goals.

6.

MANEUVERING THE PATHLESS PATH

Tattvamasi is Sanskrit for 'That you are.' It is the essence of Vedic knowledge, and literally means that we indeed are the divinity that we worship. We are mostly far from this truth, and our day-to-day existence barely correlates with this experience. Our identification with our name and form limits us to just that, a name and a form. Yoga is the craft of erasing the confines of a limited identity. The aim of yoga is to taste the exaltation that comes from identification with the boundless. It is to begin seeing the body, and its sensations and urges, as a clear separate entity from the presence that is residing and expressing as your personhood. It is seeing the beauty in being choiceless, and yet continue to play our part as though everything depends on it. This is when the meaning of the pathless path becomes clear. It means all roads are open but we are permitted to walk only on one we have been assigned. This path has no sign boards or trail markers. There is no name to this path. On the same road, the passage is different for everyone. Each one walking on this pathless path has their own journey. It's like looking into the mirror, and each finding a different reflection. There are no maps, because it can lead anywhere. There is no route, because our each move determines and crafts the next, just like in chess. To walk these few visible steps carefully, is the power allotted to us. Yoga is the art of wisely maneuvering these steps.

Find a way to receive grace gracefully.

7.

GOOD THING ABOUT BAD TIMES

Even a fragile tender babe is borne of pain, and therefore, is priceless. You can estimate the extent of torment it entails to receive God in our laps. If we do not want him, 'tis another matter. Maybe all that we really want is our sanity and happiness, with or without him. But isn't an inexhaustible resource of happiness what we call God? To achieve this, the price is pain. Without paying this price, even if God knocks at our door, we will not answer. Only suffering renders our heart's soil resilient to recognize and receive divinity. Suffering is allowed to come to us as a type of surgery of the soul, a spiritual cleansing. We are not subjected to extreme conditions merely as an act of injustice. If we look back and review times when we learnt the most, we will recall seasons of adversity, hardship, loss or distress that imparted true and lasting wisdom. After all, what do we ever gain through good times, except good times! Bad times give so much more. They chisel our propensities, lend us forbearance and grace. Above all, they enrich us with a taste of utter human helplessness, and propel us to invoke something higher. So when dark clouds hover over your head, make the most of it. Do not squander away this gift indulging in self-pity, rather try and know which lesson life is urging you to grasp. Like Ernest Hemingway said, "Forget your personal tragedy. We are all bitched by life from the start. But when you get the damned hurt, use it. Don't cheat with it."

Bad times teach us a lot.
But don't fall in love with them!

8.

ACTUALIZE YOUR POTENTIAL

Just as a lotus finds its fulfillment in bloom, and sky in a full moon night, mustn't we reach the zenith of our potential while we live, experience the whole of us and die only after having tasted the elixir of life? Be just to all the forces that came together to make *you* possible, and awaken the potentiality lying dormant within you. Unleash yourself. Reach your crescendo. Know how far you can stretch, for once. Like how fast you can run, how bright your eyes can shine, or just how quick you can manifest your thoughts. Unless you scream aloud, you may never find out how far your voice can reach! Speak to your limbs, and you will discover they have been waiting expectantly for your single utterance, your one command, to swell to their hilt. Your every cell is eager to resonate to its highest frequency. Wait no more to finally do what you always wished to do. Say the words you came to say. Train a mind equal to any emergency, and feet that keep pace with your aspiration. Let your face exude a radiance unchallenged by circumstance, and your breaths testify to the harmony that binds your body and mind. Do not regret the time you may have lost. You have an eternity to dream, and a greater eternity waits patiently for your dreams to come true.

Doubts are teasers that test our resolve.

9.

LET YOUR OPINION BE YOUR GUIDE

The world gives us an opinion, and controls us through it. Since our childhood, we have been groomed by way of rewards and punishments to choose the conduct that agrees with others. 'Don't do this' or 'do that' is mostly what we grew up with. As a consequence, gazing at faces for nods of approval becomes second nature. Apology becomes part of our psyche. We are apologetic for almost everything that we think, say or do. To live upto people's expectations of us and comply with what they think is just, we work hard, but fruitlessly. No matter how much we conform, it is always less! So stop all efforts to adhere to judgement. Refuse to accept another's estimate of you, whether good or bad. Let the world's displeasure (or pleasure) have no meaning for you. Allow your conscience to be the only yardstick of your intent, and your heart's compass be the sole authority that guides your way. Express your uniqueness, just like the constellation of stars at the time of your birth. Suit your inclinations. Stubbornly cling to what you value, in exclusion to what the world values, for in most cases it will be diametrically opposite. There is a path that has been carved exclusively for your feet to tread, a destination created just for you. Follow it unflinchingly, without seeking permission. Undertake only those actions, think only those thoughts, and be in the company of only those people who forward your highest interest—your evolution.

Stop being apologetic. If the Lord loves you as you are, what means the world!

10.

STOP POSTPONING FREEDOM—BE FREE

Bondage is not a heap of baggage to be shed one by one, but a spell of darkness that vanishes with a hint of light. Freedom is not a matter of time, but an act of audacity when you relinquish desire from your heart in one go. Few have the courage to attempt this, thus few indeed are the birds that fly beyond the sky. Know that you are the master, bound at will, giving each moment your consent to keep you chained. Each minute there is a possibility of release. You either choose it or lose it in the sands of time. There is no time to debate, weigh or negotiate. For once, try not to postpone freedom. When life stares at you with dismay, and disillusionment catches on fast like fire on dry wood, do not look away nor shut your eyes. Ask yourself, how long will you live and what is it that you truly need. The reply will be 'not for very long, and very little.' Seize this moment of truth to eliminate excess from your life, like surplus money, redundant belongings, bulky emotions, wasteful relations and overload of work. Overthrow the tyranny of undesirable habits, and debilitating thoughts. Slash the long list of objects that you aspire to own, and own to acquire more. No longer ensconce yourself in the zero risk zone, nor expect security from a life that is inherently uncertain. Tread light on your feet, and allow your soul to weigh heavy on purpose.

When freedom knocks,
have the courage to receive it.

11.

INTEND AND CREATE

Do you find it unbelievable that you, a seeming mere speck of creation, causes everything that stirs? Or that you sway situations, attract fortunes and misfortunes, fulfillment and denials to finally materialize the cosmos you want. If you are alert, you will recognize each instance in life as something you always asked for. From the shape of your toenail, scent of your skin, size of your room, script of your life, to the characters enacting as friends and foes—everything is tailored to your request. We are responsible for each and every dialogue that we deliver, and every discourse that we hear from life. Delve in your heart, and you shall know it is true. You can command fate if you merely become aware of your own creativity at play. It is a universe of thought, and you can create what you want by the same raw ingredient. Merely divert your thought energy to where you wish to go in physical reality. Think about it clearly and often, and you will be irresistibly drawn there, without a choice. Effortlessly, you will unfetter the saga of desires captured in your being. Key is not to try; just will. Let what you want, want you. The more silent and detached you are, the faster events will transpire. Know that the world exists for you. It cannot fail its own cause of creation. So it is time to be unafraid and tell life, 'I am ready. Give me all that you got.'

Resolve builds galaxies, shapes planets, and lends light to stars.

12.

BEFRIEND THE LAWS OF LIFE

As we grow in years, so does our distrust. Caution mounts. Innocence gives way to suspicion. Curiosity melts into an 'I've seen it all' stance. Wrinkles of resignation begin to erupt in our contours, for now we trust life to only bring us the promise of demise. All this, because all this while, we swam against the tide of life, and flouted its principles, rather than moving in consensus. Life connotes giving, we believe in taking, demanding, snatching. Life means acceptance. We do just the opposite, frown at what we have, and what we have not. Life is about living the moment, but from *this* moment we are always absent! Thus, in our defiance against the very pillars of existence, we stand no ground, and slowly but crumble. Rather, life gives up on us, death embraces. Key to eternity is to befriend life, and apply its ground rules to everyday living. Take recourse in its magnanimity, feel secure in the folds of its uncertainty. Most importantly, take up the challenge of 'not knowing' again. Courage to return to innocence. You stand only to gain by loosening your hold on the experience and belief of age. Wisdom lies in catching life's pulse, decoding its secret language, and making its laws our own, so that life becomes a perpetual companion, and one conquers the myth of dying.

Live, for the sake of pure play.

13.

MOVEMENT IS THE MANTRA

When it's time to do something, don't wait, because time does not wait. It moves faster than our intentions. This is a great lesson to learn from time, the art of moving. Time is perpetually in motion, and that's what makes it eternal and timeless. It is a tough one to catch and enslave, as it doesn't stay in one place for long. Stopping for it would mean death, nobody will let it go! Time never stops, and neither should we, for we are a creature of time. When we stop, we stagnate. When we stop, attachment and greed become friends. So make a move in each moment. Do not stop at an object, an emotion, an attachment or infatuation. However, employing movement for transformative growth is an art. Most of us retain who we are in toto, no matter where we go. We give away things, but rarely who we are. We change residences, but rarely ourselves. The familiar, the known, the comfortable, is the start of rusting, the beginning of descent. It douses our curiosity, garbs our vulnerability, compromises our preparedness, and of course our intelligence, because it's simply not needed anymore! The jump can only begin to happen, when we are willing to let each new place, perspective or posture be like stoking the fire. It must reveal a unique side of us with each turn. Embark on an exploration with a difference, in a conscious seeking mode, wherein senses are not to be entertained but stilled.

Soak in the journey;
the destination is a myth.

14.

INTROSPECT TO RESOLVE CONFLICT

We expend phenomenal amounts of energy in outward quest, and waste precious intent. Spend as much time as you may in evading yourself, one day you will have to but relent. Reality will finally dawn, that war or peace, events first happen inside of you before they precipitate externally. Like symptoms of a disease. You are the cause, rest just a consequence. You are the deterministic factor, not the stars, planetary postures or destiny. Notice that when you harbor fear, you often encounter what you dread. And when you are in harmony, you are rewarded with supporting circumstances. It is easy to look outside, tough to focus within, but this is precisely what we need practice—solemn introspection. Start questioning the very foundation of your thinking, your beliefs. Dissect your hitherto unchallenged assumptions in the laboratory of your mind, and pin them up against truth. Interrogate and defeat all ideology through sheer will and objectivity, not caring it is your own. Trace every thought to whence it came, and soon you shall arrive at emptiness, the stuff you are made of. You begin to feel by intuition that you are the divine current running the show, the energy that has raised you from a fetus to a child, youth and adult. This realization resolves all conflict. You realize that choosing is a myth, and dabbling in dispute between two choices is like playing with a mirage. Futile!

The beloved sits in our bosom,
awaiting our return.

15.

DETACHED INVOLVEMENT IS YOGA

Yoga is not just about certain postures or breath control (though they serve as aids), but a practice of calmness in face of provocation, and restraint in the hour of temptation. Yoga is not the prerogative of saints or ascetics either, but a way of life more critical for a person of the world to adopt. It does not imply denial, rather moderation in extremities of emotion. It is about being stationed in the middle, to that point of equilibrium that we always cross while swinging to extremes. To derive real fulfillment from life, let the essential part of you never get swayed from this center. Remain in the middle lane, and impartially watch the traffic whizz past on either side. Live with detachment, practice being aloof yet involved, as though the script is running through you, not *to* you. With the needle of detachment, pluck out the fine invisible and invasive threads of attachment, that penetrate our soul skin deep. With illusory detachment, uproot illusory attachment. It may appear in contradiction, but total detachment implies complete involvement. When we no longer invest our soul in anything, we are fully alert and efficient. We stand to lose nothing, for what we are cannot be lost in any gamble. We give totally, for we want nothing in return. Now the graph of our emotions becomes a straight line, and we are in yoga! *Vairagya* (detachment) indeed is the boat with which we can move about freely in the ocean of *saṃsāra*. Without this boat, one most certainly drowns.

All attachment is diversion
from straight path home.

16.

TAP INTO INNER STILLNESS

Indeed, silence soothes, inspires and comforts more than words. True conversations happen speechlessly. The finest teachings are conveyed when our lips are sealed and minds rested. The space of awareness from which we have emerged as sparks of a great fire, is silent. The stuff we have sprung from is made of deep tranquility. The farther we go into this silence, the more profound are the verses that spring from our lips. To commune with our source, we must still ourselves. Accessing this domain of stillness is not complicated, and most certainly does not lie in intellectual reasoning, philosophical debates or occult experiences. Silence is the only way to silence. Cultivate stillness. Be willing to still desire. Keep a watch over your mind. Initially your head may whirl with unstoppable thoughts, and dense clouds of confusion may block your vision. But as you persist in your sincerity to get emptied, you will find yourself moving from the noise on the periphery to the center of the circle, to that point of serenity inside of you where there is a surge of unconditional bliss. Gradually, gaps between thoughts get prolonged. Subtle truths, that are beyond the grasp of the intellect, uncover. Solutions to riddles spring up. Retreating to stillness will never isolate you from your near ones, nor get you out of sync with the world. In fact, every dip into silence would result in greater harmony and peace.

*When you have a lot to say,
become silence.*

17.

LOVE YOURSELF UNCONDITIONALLY

We love our children and pets unconditionally, but rarely our own self. Finding one reason or another to fault ourselves, we move about carrying a satchel of self-condemnations. End this dichotomy between what you are, and what you should be. Accept yourself today, unequivocally, without a cause or explanation. Adore yourself, as much as when you obey, as when you defy the rules, and equally when you triumph and when you fail. Do not wait till tomorrow or a perfect you, to espouse your cause. You can be inconsistent, indecisive, chaotic, lazy or not as young, yet you are deserving of care. More importantly, who would uphold you if you reproach yourself? Respect the phenomenon which is you, irrespective of the many anomalies. Perhaps, the whole business of attaining realization is about giving up notions of impeccability, and embracing your person in entirety. Be no longer caught in what could have been or should be. Stop seeking mirrors to assure you of your beauty, and notice your countenance change shade completely. You begin to glisten with ease, as self-consciousness fades away. You become radiant in your naturalness, total in the expression of who you are. On an occasion, when even the evil voice in your head is heard not with rebuke but compassion, the sky is set clear for the sun to shine.

Perception is the only reality.

18.

REVIVE YOUR BOND WITH DIVINITY

What is your relationship with God, or the law that governs life? How often do you relate as a rebellious child, a servile aide, and how rarely as a pal or a lover? Know that whatever link you establish, the law reciprocates, mirroring your advance. When you ascribe attributes of an account keeper, God keeps records. When you look up to him, he has to but look down upon you. When you avoid him, he shuns you. When you extend your hand like a comrade, he holds it and walks with you like one. See a lover in him, and you witness the law turn partial for your sake! Choice of how you wish to bond with your creator is yours, but revive your connection with your source. That's who you would call upon during the final moments of life. Imagine knocking at a door you haven't visited in years. What kind of certainty would you have that your call will be answered? The time to start investing in this link, is now. Demolish the power equation, and barter. Just ask, and do not doubt that you shall receive. In actuality, you give to yourself. Who else would? Just as a speck of light *is* light, you are *that*. There are no two. When you bow, you revere your own Self. When you confess, you beg for your own pardon. When you pray, you ask for your own consent to happiness, and burn incense to your own divinity. You are the ethereal one, hiding from and seeking your own glory. Give up this sobriety, and return to supremacy.

The moment that can free you comes every moment.

19.

NATURE IS OUR TRUE SOUL MATE

Searching for soul mates is a reflection of the universal theme of duality. It is a mystical journey of finding one's own reflection in another vessel. While it is speculative whether soul mates exist or not, there is one mate we have that is inseparable. That is nature. We arise from *panchabhoota,* the five elements of fire, water, earth, air and space. We live encased in them, and we dissolve unto them. Nature indeed is our soul mate, and when treated as such, offers unconditional support and reciprocity. The direction of breeze, whistling of birds, humming of insects, and showers of rain are all cues that are imparted to its lovers. Have you ever seen a cloud drift by and assume a strange shape just when you were looking? These are far from coincidences. Each little twist in nature's mood has a message. Not needlessly have wandering monks languished in forests, and by no means were they alone during their retreat on secluded mountaintops. They were in perpetual communion with the most compassionate, intelligent and wise companion one can hope for. Enrich yourself by winning nature's friendship, establish a rapport with its elements. Decode the language of thrashing ocean waves. Start a dialogue with the seasons, sunrises and sunsets. Read your imprint on wet mud, and your reflection in dew drops. You will soon discover that nature is not just our soul's mate for an eternity, it is also our preceptor. All of its manifestations have a teaching to impart.

Dreams are trail markers.
Follow them to stay on the way.

20.

TREAT NATURE AS GURU

There is a lot of wisdom and joy to be acquired from nature, and its many creations. A house with the background humming of insects, and pigeons cuddling together, is a happy home. Joyous chirping of birds at radiant dawns and quiet sun sets are refreshing sounds worth dialing into. Besides being great company, and source of catharsis, living in proximity with animals and birds imparts valuable lessons, if we observe them keenly. Dattatreya, the Adi Guru (first teacher) whose disciple was Shiva himself, had twenty four preceptors in nature. Noteworthy amongst these are the earth, that represents dharma; the wind symbolizes freedom of truth. The sun, moon and ocean emphasize the unchanging nature of life. The sky stands for the infinite Self. The spider reminds one of the transient nature of material world. The moth, elephant, and deer guide against the overwhelming distraction caused by desire. The honeybee warns against worldly attachments. The python emphasizes the benefits of simple living, as it uses only abandoned places as home. Elements of fire and water show the path to purify the contamination of materialism. The caterpillar teaches that one can reach godhood, by sheer concentration. Fish are constantly awake and watchful. Birds possess nothing, and receive just as much as they need. Observe, and absorb teachings directly from nature and her humble creatures. In some ways, they seem to know the secret.

Attachment is one disease we are
all afflicted with, yet do not seek a cure.

21.

PLAY THE GAME OF LIFE TO WIN

At every turn, life throws a challenge, proposes a war, wherein one of the two must happen. Our triumph or defeat. Life wishes to lead us to a point where it no longer matters whether we win or lose, but we have to win to reach that point! Till life poses as an opponent, we must respond as one. If little squirrels can take on the challenge of winning against predators, why not we? We are not exempt from the rules of the game, and we must play to win. Firstly, stop expecting denials and obstructions from the universe. More often than not, we are our own hindrance to success than anyone else. Victory often lands at our doorstep effortlessly, when we overcome our resistance to win. Be total. Totality is a pre-requisite in war, just like in love. Aim at conquering the mind of the adversary (often yourself), not individual moves, for oft you may mess up the moves, yet win the game. Play fearlessly. Do not assume as threats, situations that are indeed opportunities. Keep your cool. When you appear to have been overthrown, you can still overcome, if you do not yield to helplessness disguised as prayer, but offer to be your own help. Often for a true feat, you have to rise from your debris, not from the pedestal of good fortune. You must not surrender when you can surmount! Always think ahead, the next step, forgetting the previous. Play to your own conviction. Then, even if you fail, you would have succeeded.

Fight when you know you cannot win.
When victory is certain, resign!

22.

CONTENTMENT ITSELF IS LIBERATION

It is true that unless we are wholesome from within, we cannot make another joyous, far succeed at creating any worthwhile miracles in our life. When we are joyful and content, competence and excellence follow. On the contrary, if we build behavioral perfection on a weak foundation of discontentment and disease, then our superfluously acquired virtues disintegrate at the slightest provocation. How does one achieve this shift from discontentment to contentment? How does one cover this distance from falsity to truth, darkness to light, and misery to rapture? Ask yourself, what needs to happen before you are happy. And know, that till such time something needs to occur before you smile, you continue to be miserable. Soon after your first condition to happiness is met, another crops up. This cycle goes on indefinitely, till you lose in the bargain exactly what you sought. Life is too short for postponement of happiness. Without relying on the next instance, learn to be blissful now, and to be blissful now, let your joy be unconditional. Do not base it on the presence or absence of something or somebody in your life. Make an unconditional commitment to happiness and say, that 'today, as I am, whatsoever life offers me, I am happy, I am content.' Then, desirable situations may or may not follow (though you have set the climate to attract them), but you would have achieved a prime goal of life, in the present moment.

Happiness that is insubordinate to circumstance, is called bliss.

23.

CHOOSE JOY OVER SORROW

Life is too precious to be whiled away in trivia. Each moment is a treasure, a gift from the beyond, an opportunity for us to experience our own grandeur. Each second we are given a rebirth, a chance to rejoice. Yet we miss it, taking life for granted. Secretly knowing, that giving is the index of true fulfillment, we silently say to ourselves 'today I can be selfish, tomorrow I shall be selfless' or 'today I can receive, tomorrow I shall return.' How can we be sure that life will give us that one chance to be magnanimous? With the certainty of death, the promise of the end, where is the time to hold back or the space to hoard? We know not how many lifetimes we have suffered, how many moments we have murdered in dreary, how much emotion we have wasted on the inconsequential. Who also knows how much time is left of our journey. Yet, we know one thing for sure, that this instance is ours, and we are alive to capture our goals, seize our desires, and give back to others what we have received. Be alert. Do not waste a single moment. Cherish it. Drink it! Do not let it pass without giving you its due. Allow it not to fool you into ignorance, or cheat you into slumber. Let cooperation rise above competition, faith surmount skepticism, and love reign over animosity. Choose joy over sorrow, giving over taking. As a bud spontaneously bursts into flower, blossom to embrace all those in your vicinity.

Let the good in you rise during bad times.

24.

EMERGE FROM YOUR POINT OF PURITY

Sometimes life compels us to find a cave inside of us, that is more secure and solitary than the Himalayas, more fragrant than the wild flowers growing in the deep woods. This is a place where there are no shopping malls, hangout joints, families or things to do list. This center is our home, our rest. Like a lullaby, it stills all turbulence. It contains in seed the great secret. Find this center, this point of purity within yourself. Search for it in every nook of what you call *you*. It must subsist somewhere, despite all the noise we have created. Every once in a while, get away from present callings, and explore the most intimate attitudes towards yourself. Confront yourself totally. You will discover then, that behind the maddening chaos surrounding you, there exists eternal order within. You start becoming aware of little movements you were previously unaware of, like blinking of eyes, gulping of throat, and your breath. You will learn newer ways of doing same things, refreshing ways of loving. Having found this center, train yourself to dive in at will and emerge from its order, peace and silence to operate in the world, play your part, and fulfill your destiny.

Guard your purity from idle talk.

25.

BUILDING SOUL CHARACTER

Understand, that one component we have been granted for transformation is we ourselves, never the other. Only though self-reform can we hope to mould others. Thus, when you spot shortcomings in your person, be intolerant of them. Do not fight them, but with discernment, reverse their flow. For instance, when anger visits, welcome it but direct it towards your imperfections. When greed knocks, do not ask it to leave, rather be extremely greedy for the highly selfish endeavor of self-enhancement. Resent, but your own self, for not being able to pierce the illusion completely. Compete, but with the phenomenon which is you, and constantly lead yourself higher, and further on. When in doubt, compel yourself to trust. In this manner, achieve supremacy over undesirable elements of your personality. When confronted with quirks of others, be extremely tolerant. Just as while preparing a meal, we need the knife, the cutting board and all spices in correct portion, only such individuals and situations arise in our life space that chisel our propensities. Once you understand this divine design, you will welcome friends, but never let go of critics. At the cost of appearing nasty, they give you invaluable aid. More importantly, obsessing with faults of others lowers our psychic immunity, and makes us vulnerable to absorbing those very traits in our own person. That is, assuming we already don't have them! After all, we can only recognize something if it exists in us. Acknowledge this fundamental fact, drop judgement, and busy yourself in clearing your own garden.

Let good intent be your only shield.

26.

FIX YOUR MIND ON THE HIGHEST IDEAL

Path of personal evolution is not an easy one. The evil in man is strong enough to prevent it! Soon after we make a conscious effort to rise above our limitations, more arise. Rather, we become more keenly aware of those that were there all along. It is heartbreaking to resolve to live differently, act from a higher awareness and consciousness. And then watch oneself slide helplessly with the force of habit, as the smaller self clamors for attention. In our half-understood reality of the space-time continuum, it is indeed hard to hold onto flickering glimpses of truth. Understanding that this struggle is not our lone quest, but the plight of all those who have striven, brings consolation. The thought that our unique struggles, downfalls and embarrassments are not really that unique, brings relief, and inspiration to carry on. In moments of self-loathing for having failed, practice having compassion for yourself. Know that limitations borne out of an egoistic sense of self, even though ghastly and innumerable, are transient appearances, mere images floating on mind's surface. Our true nature remains unchanged. Our original purity has remained untainted, despite the myriad of ego projections. After all, how can a finite ego and its pranks spoil the grandeur of the Self! You are at best a dreamer who has gotten lost in the dream. Your limitations too, are an imagination.

Don't waste your striving
on what comes and goes.

27.

POSSESS COURAGE—NEED LITTLE ELSE

Courage is one word that needs no introduction. When it surges, in spite of sorrow you smile, and despite decline, you rise. Courage is one boon that makes up for the absence of all others. There is nothing in this world superior to it. With the company of courage, you are equipped for life and prepared for death. You can endure desertion and downfall with the same goodwill, as you would bear a fortune. What is courage? Living without protecting our self-interest is courage, as it requires placing endless trust in nature to provide for your needs. Vulnerability is courage, when you are no longer afraid to be hurt, robbed or cheated. Complete expression of who you are is intense bravery. You indeed are gallant, when unconcerned about a critical opinion, you express your sentiments fully, explore your sensitivities to the hilt, and recognize your emotions honestly. Love by nature is courageous, for it is not afraid of rejection. An act of trust is an act of courage, it's like the free fall. It does not doubt that a hand would leap forth to save, and it mostly does! Above all, living in the world untainted by desire, is the supreme act of audacity. To inculcate this shade of courage, understand that nothing can be snatched away from you, for you truly possess nothing. Realize that nothing can be added to you, for you lack nothing. What you are, can neither be increased nor diminished. For you lack nothing, you require nothing, and when you desire nothing, you fear nothing. The world calls it courage. You know it is just your natural state of being!

Walk fearlessly, and you walk safe.

28.

TRUTH IS TRULY COURAGEOUS

Truth has enormous courage. When you are by its side, you are enormously strong. Whereas in the camp of untruth, no matter how many weapons you gather, how many feats you acquire, or how many accolades you may receive, your foundation is extremely fragile. You are fickle, and very weak. Your confidence is nothing but disguised arrogance. On the surface, everything may appear to be going well with you life, but you have no idea how life is making a mockery of you. You have no clue that with one whiff of a whimsical breeze, your confidence could be reduced to rubble. When you are in the wing of falsehood, your flamboyance is without true purport, your demeanor is ignorant. Like the demon king Ravana in epic Ramayana, one may succeed in acquiring many boons by the power of (misdirected) penance, but will eventually be overthrown by the symbol of righteousness, Lord Rama. Stand for truth. Oppose and destroy all that is inconsistent, and contrary to righteousness in your own person. Rise actively against all those forces that aim to destroy your inherent goodness. Side with integrity, have virtue as your comrade. Then, your foundation will become so strong that no wind of fate shall ever take away from you what you rightly deserve. You would no longer need to protect your interest, as the heavenly angels labor to defend your might.

Let truth be your only valor.
Love, your only shame.

29.

WHY FLAP WHEN YOU CAN FLOAT

Indeed, the whole notion of effort is a myth, a falsehood. In truth, we have been given no work to do. We are on an eternal holiday, only we can't believe it. We foolishly devote our lives to working hard, and still harder. We have probably worked so hard by now, and gotten so habitual to straining, that we do not let go of the leash in our hand, even though it may clamp our own neck. We are also beginning to find not striving very difficult! Tell me, did we exert to be born and grow to this height? To what degree of certainty can we determine if we shall see tomorrow, or even the whole of today? The earth, without demanding, gets the sunshine it needs. Birds, without hoarding, get the grain they require. Can't we place the same trust in the universe to give us what we deserve, and stop believing for once, that our hankering has a bearing on our share? The world is a playground, and it's always playtime. Spontaneously, trustingly, like a child, drop all effort. Dropping anything is easier than latching onto it. It is the holding on that is difficult. Just like dying is easy, it's the clutching to life that makes it seem difficult. Giving is so much easier than restraining, also more joyful. Trusting is easier than doubting, and much simpler. Likewise, letting go isn't a defeat, it's a win-win, it's the start of fun. The moment you drop the pot of honey that you are clasping, all greedy flies too, go along with it, allowing you to savor the real nectar. 'Tis sweeter than it sounds.

When everything seems to fall in place,
know that it was already so.

30.

RENOUNCE SENSE OF DOERSHIP

Without sacrifice, there is no reward. In the world of the spirit, the sacrifice that is asked of us is ultimate. We are asked to renounce the sense of doer-ship that we carry with us all the time, even in sleep. "Though all actions are done by the constituents of nature, the ignorant one, deluded by his egoism, regards himself as the doer," says the Bhagavad Gita. From where and when did we acquire this habit we cannot say, but taking ownership of actions is at the root of misery, and relentless cycles of births and deaths. No matter how many sacred rituals we perform, how many scriptures or postures we master, or how many pilgrimages we rub our feet on, the day we eradicate this sense will be the day that frees us. It is indeed the hardest to shed, but the rewards that follow are befitting. The journey is excruciating in the beginning, as the sense of 'I' begins to recede. Our whole sense of survival depends on it. Giving it up, or being made to feel powerless is the most humbling experience one can have. Yet, doing deeds in the spirit of renunciation alone is the way. While engaged in action, operate with detachment, and surrender all actions to the divine principle. This is the only means to attain liberation. As we stick to this yogic renunciation, and keep sacrificing sense of ownership from our life, we get to view some spectacular landscapes in the spirit world.

*In this world where nothing is real,
play with images!*

31.

HOW LESS IS MORE

When we haven't eaten for days, a glass of milk fills us to the brim. After days of fasting, a glass of plain water becomes more than enough. Likewise, for someone who has abstained from company, someone who has been solitary for days, a brief hello or verbal exchange is a lot. Too much in fact. It takes time to wash off. When we give up somethings, their space inside of us begins to shrink, just like our stomachs. A contraction occurs, a receding, and less becomes a lot more. This principle works with everything. It works with thoughts, with the words we utter, with the work we do, and with all our needs and desires. Nothing and no one is indispensable. That's precisely how yogis can survive on mere sunlight. They have done away with all types of need a long time ago. Air, sunlight, water, feel of earth underneath the feet, that's truly a lot for them. The less we use, the less we need, and our definition of indulgence changes. One begins to clearly see that sin is nothing but layers and layers of unnecessary luggage, that we have been towing this long. It is sin, because it slows us down on this mission of life, when what is needed is mental and physical agility. It is sin, because it makes us ill-eqippped for the battle of life. An intelligent mind is one that deploys itself to skillfully eliminate the needless, and retain only those featherlight thought impressions, that carry us forward on our path.

We get linked to things we own,
like a blood bond.

32.

BECOMING A SOLITAIRE

Most of us know what it is to be solitary. It is having a lot to say but no one to hear. It is desiring a lot but getting only one— yourself. Being solitary is much more than this. A moment spent in its jaws of appalling isolation and emptiness, is like a lifetime suffered. There is an instinctive urge to run away from it. If in this moment, you do not escape but meet this void, rather understand that you *are* this void, then surfaces a sense of aloneness. In this sense of aloneness, there is no fear. You no longer shun yourself, you are no longer scared. The great abyss envelops you, and you become full in its emptiness. You are complete, content by your reflection, overwhelmed by your presence. You have journeyed from being solitary to becoming a solitaire. By giving others company, you grant them a favor! True solitaires are free beings, bound at will. Their strength is masked by unassuming resilience, their brilliance is veiled by everyday demeanor. They possess nothing, yet make you envious of their wealth. They utter not a word, yet say much. Stepping by their side gives the calm one draws from a silent lake. More and more you wish to be with such a one, who seems to require not even the ground he rests upon. This supreme state of grandeur awaits our arrival at its threshold. We are intended to be solitaires in this world mine!

Solitude frees us of the burden
of conditioned identity.

33.

ATTITUDE OF SOLITUDE

Solitude is the sister of yoga. Without a mind seeped in solitude, most practices yield only superfluous results. With every beckoning of externality, we find ourselves sway. Solitude shields us from getting sucked into a world of illusion, by keeping us rooted in our center. Being in solitude does not imply one is alone. It simply means one is in one's own company! It is just a different kind of togetherness, wherein you tune in to your innermost friend, the companionship of your own Self. You drop your social masks and be unabashedly you. You become acutely aware of your thoughts, and cognizant of the sound of your breath. Your awareness becomes so heightened, that it's difficult to tell if you are on the verge of enlightenment or death! Being in solitude could initially seem painful to some, but with patient practice, it begins to spell something immensely liberating. Your past begins to converse with you, and buried memories stir up. You recall things you forgot to say, tasks you forgot to complete, and values you held most dear. Resolutions spring up, and riddles begin to get solved. Whether you laugh, weep, sing, dance, or merely stay ensconced in the simplicity of existing, you get a chance to revive a rapport with yourself. With practice, solitude would become an attitude, a perspective to live, wherein our dependence on other people and externality reduces. One is content with very little, just oneself!

To be tethered, you need another.
To be free—just yourself!

34.

BURN FULLY—LEAVE NO RESIDUE

The sight of eunuchs sends waves of discomfort up our spine. One wonders how they are so self-assured in a state of dichotomy, not realizing that we are much already there, a degree more self-assured in our perpetual state of vacillation. We can be aptly described in terms of ratios, for we are never really hundred per cent. We are lukewarm lovers, safe risk takers, cynical believers, restrained givers, insipid hopers, and modest competitors. We are passive onlookers of the real performers. Being partially afflicted in our expression, we never exceed the ordinary, the usual, the expected. Though well versed with the dilemma of the middle class, mid-life crisis and plight of middlemen, we treat our condition quite lightly. Admiring life from a middle distance, we never go to the brink for a face-to-face. The golden mean can get killing sometimes, like the time gap between ignition and explosion. When such a moment dawns, that you get tired of being bifurcated, and wish to experience the relief of extremism, gauge which side you weigh more, even slightly. Shift your weight there at once. Take a leap. Own a stand. Give up your half nelson hold on life. Remember, totality does not mean excess. While excess is an overdoing without use of discernment, totality is a state of mind when less becomes more than enough!

*When you feel something
is missing, it's probably you.*

35.

QUESTION YOUR EXISTENCE

We all search for answers, without asking the right questions. Ask, if the proof of your existence is merely a rising and falling breath, persistent pangs of hunger, and beads of sweat that sprout on your brow. If you are told that you exist in spite of all these, that you are not the one who ages and dies, do not believe it. Question it. Believe only your experience, your own truth. Never borrow understanding. Invoke your own! Question incessantly the plight of being encased in folds of flesh, torn by polarities, chased by ghosts of empty ambition. Do not play this futile game of wits anymore. Persistently enquire what your purpose is. For once, know who you really are, why you are here, and where do you belong. Discover your origins. Start questioning what you know, and discard unverified beliefs. It is true that we are timeless. Yet, it's also true that our stay on this planet is timed. The body will drop one day, and till the illusion of time exists, time exists. To pierce this illusion, there is very little time! Hasten to set yourself free. Like a horse with blinkers, who sees just one goal post ahead, focus all your striving at the sole burning quest of self-knowledge. Ask only this one question, till the knowledge finally exudes in your being, that you were and will always be.

Don't wait. Nothing's around the bend.

36.

WHY THE WISE ACT FOOL

Beauty of life is that everything exists at the same time, concurrently. Everything also exists in pair of opposites, like beauty and filth, joy and grief, treason and loyalty. Music and noise are a matter of opinion. Whatever is said is always relative, and thus in error. All opinions play on the rim of polarity. The moment we voice one perspective, we dispute the other. Opinions are also like chameleon, they change over time. They are fickle and frivolous. They are a symptom of the ego, a purging of personality. Even desires are opinions, and have no real substance; they too change over time. The reason why the wise stay quiet or act fools, is because they know that they don't know. It's others who call them wise. They merely listen to the roar of the waves, as sounds emerging from the same ocean. They mean either nothing or the same thing. Following this line of thought, you will arrive at the conclusion that there is no reason to engage in any argument at all. If we were to drop one opinion a day, how much lighter we would be in a week! Dropping the load of opinions is akin to catching the pulse of our ego identity, and rendering it powerless. Capturing and destroying one's personhood in totality is difficult. Catching hold of opinions and discarding them is easier. So start eliminating these seemingly harmless opinions one by one, by not taking them too seriously. Whatever you think you know, kill it.

When you think, you lose the way.

37.

ART OF LOOKING WITHIN

We are in a deep sleep of ignorance, a spell of darkness. We are guests in the tent of *maya,* and have been served the liquor of illusion. We are looking into the mirror, and merging with the image that is flimsy, wavering, and most importantly, unreal. Glimpses of truth are rare, and promptly brushed aside or forgotten, as though we have vowed to mate with falsity. No one can rescue us from this illusory appearance of the phenomenal world, because it is our own creation. Through individual effort alone, can we hope to dismantle it. World's resolve is to draw us out, and our resolve must be to retreat within. Closing our eyes to the external world is stressed in all religions, yet the real practice is to look within with open eyes. Indeed, looking at the eye, one can tell if one has begun the inner pilgrimage or still wandering on the periphery. Eyes of a newborn, that of a dying man, a realized saint or madmen look just the same. They are vacant, lost to the void. Unless you have pledged to devote endless lifetimes to a sleep state—strive to awaken, with a firm determination to end all dreaming. The art of looking within is to discern the real from the unreal, and identify those images in the lake of your mind that exert the most control over you. Then, shrug them off like a leech sucking your blood, a thief stealing your money, or a magician enticing you with tricks. See through the play, and let it recede, as a nightmare departs at the crack of dawn.

Ask yourself, and you would know.
Wait, and you shall wait forever.

38.

CONQUEST OF THE GREAT ILLUSION

Lord Krishna says in the Bhagavad Gita, "My *maya* is hard to cross. Her way of operating is perverse. She makes the real seem unreal, consciousness appear like matter, God appear like man, and the one many." We are indeed like little children, estranged from our home of eternity, lost to a land of impermanence and fantasy. We are stranded in the maze of multiplicity. Dramas of victories and losses, themes of loving and parting keep us enamored. Patanjali points out how ignorant it is to take the non-eternal, impure non-Self to be pure and eternal. The lack of awareness of reality, egoism, attractions, repulsions and strong desire for life are the five-fold causes of misery. Yet, like a bee stuck to the honey of desire, we are unable to escape. What is the way to overcome infatuation with the myriad forms of infatuation? When a thin invisible veil is the enemy, denial is not the solution to render it powerless. Vigil is. Uninterrupted practice of awareness of the real, remembering *Shivoham* or 'I am not apart from Shiva' (the changeless, formless, all pervading principle) is the only means to disperse this mirage. Withdrawal of the mind from distractions, and knowing that transcendence exists at all times, even in our deluded state, eventually results in the conquest of the great illusion.

Only the one who has won over infatuation, is fit for liberation.

39.

MUSE ON LIFE'S IMPERMANENCE

"The years of a lifetime are like a flash of lightning. Even if you care about the nose hung in front of your face, still be careful and each moment work for enlightenment," said Dōgen, the famous Japanese Zen master. These lines drive home the message with a jolt, as to how carelessly we treat time, and how recklessly misplaced is our attention. The serious involvement with which we enact in the world is deserving of pity, considering how ephemeral life really is. Our body, our mind, our perspectives, our relationships and situations are constantly in a state of flux, and finally simply vanish. Whatever we hold in our palm slips out, and all that we touch turns to dust, in a matter of while. If we could bow in front of this inherent impermanence every single day, we would live differently. The whole texture of our life would change. The task that pleads urgent application, is constant alertness to the perishable, and rigorous effort to arrive at the permanent. Reminding yourself that 'this too is unreal' and 'this too shall pass' in fortune and adversity, hope and despair, in fact with every pair of opposites that presents before us, is one practice that will never fail you. As you let the truth of the transient dawn, your gaze may get transfixed on that which never changes.

Thank God you have
another day to prepare for death.

40.

DETECT ONENESS IN DUALITY

One practice of Vedanta is to be mindful of the polarity in all circumstances. When you experience gratification, know that there is starvation somewhere. When you encounter hatred, perceive the flicker of love in the same pair of eyes. Do not try and change anything. Just be aware that till there is light, shade exists. Lurking behind every woman is a man, and just as the adult resides in a newborn, the grave throbs in pulsating youth. Discern the unmistakable duality at all times, like the contradiction in consensus, and conclusion contained at the start. The whole world will then begin to appear as a *pas de deux*, a step of two, or a split seed. Close your eyes and reflect on this. Ask yourself what is it that is whole, that does not have an antithesis. Seek, in the sphere of your heart, the sacred word that does not have an antonym. You will know, then, that all apparent division and polarity is illusive. There exists no separation. We are one indivisible whole, operating from a single source, sewn from a single thread of consciousness. The seeming conflict between spiritual and material, realism and fantasy, destiny and will, is a ghost. In truth, there are no answers, for there aren't any questions. Life is pure living, a frivolous play of consciousness, a dance of divinity casting shadows of name and form. There ain't no seriousness to this sport!

You alone are. All else is a shadow.

Part Two

MEDITATIONS

41.

BHAKTI—YOGA OF LOVE

What you think you become, emphasized the Buddha. It is indeed true. We not only attract what we consistently think about, we become it. Our mind begins to act like a magnet, and attract the objects of our attention, as well as imbibe their traits (energy frequencies). Herein lies the danger, as well as opportunity. That absorption, wherein the chosen object of attention is God is called *bhakti* yoga. Lovers of the divine say that on this path of yoga, it is only a matter of time that the lover becomes the loved, and worshipper becomes the worshipped. Bhakti yoga is the simplest method of arriving at divine unity. The trek on love's terrain is way more scenic than the rough roads of reason. On this path of yoga, strenuous postures, complex breathing techniques or intellectual debates have no place. Unlike other branches of yoga, bhakti cannot be practiced, nor forced. The seed is sown in each one of us, and comes to bloom when the season is right. When devotion blossoms, remembrance becomes a constant companion. This remembrance is not always about singing divine glory or chanting; it's a longing for the inexplicable. At other times, it expresses as a divine restlessness, and makes one wander. In advanced stages of absorption, it pulls you into meditative trance-like states. Transformation ensues, and gradually, we start to resonate with the frequency of the object of our worship.

Absorption is the disease, as well as the cure.

42.

USE MANTRAS TO STILL THE MIND

Rhythm and harmony are intrinsic to nature. To align ourselves with this harmony, we must catch its rhythm. One potent method is to chant mantras, or sacred syllables whose sound vibrations penetrate layers of our psyche, and eventually still inner discord. Though ideally received from a living ascended master, do not wait for initiation. Select your mantra intuitively, going by the deity you relate with. Chant with the rosary of your breath (cycle of breathing), such that not a single breath passes without the Name. Slowly, as the mantra gets rooted, the chant drops from your lips to your heart, and acts as a lullaby to the mind. Whatever deity you call upon, call with love. Listen to its echo. Visualize the syllable forming a protective armor around you. Put your soul in each turn of the rosary. Let your heart sweat with fervor with every inhalation and exhalation. Such constant remembrance at dawn and at dusk yields enormous result. As the momentum of the chant builds up, vultures of darkness get destroyed, negativities melt away. Strength and detachment become a way of life. If you persist with this practice, you would begin to taste the nectar described by Sufi Hāfez, "Happiest were the times spent with the beloved. Rest were vain and fruitless."

Our deepest desire is to meet God.

43.

ART OF BECOMING RESOLUTE

We must ultimately become what we idealize. This is the science behind glorifying idols of gods and goddesses in various religions. However, to truly benefit from such worship, we must decode the symbolism hidden in their mystical form. Image of Ganesha is loaded with esoteric meaning. He is the presiding deity of *muladhara* chakra, the first energy center (out of seven) we must unlock on our uphill climb to self-realization. Different forms of Ganesha have different meanings, but common elements are the trunk, the big belly, the tusk, and the mouse. Elephant head on a human body is not as innocent as it appears. It stands for strength, will power, and intellectual finesse to discern mystical realms. The conspicuously large belly stands for fully consuming, and not rejecting the experiences we invite in this life. The extraordinarily large ears and head point to the importance of listening and reflection as a means of acquiring wisdom. The single tusk urges us to stay one-pointed, and focused on our spiritual quest of overcoming duality. Ganesha's standing pose on one leg advises that we allow one aspect of our personality to deal with the world, while firmly rooting the other in self-enquiry. The mouse represents desire, and the axe promises its destruction. The rope promises to rescue us from bondage, and the lotus in Ganesha's hand lures us to the supreme goal of liberation. Finally, the platter of sweets at Ganesha's feet represents the reward of spiritual pursuit. It is auspicious to meditate on Ganesha before initiating any work, as his energy vibration removes all roadblocks to progress.

*It is a worshipful moment when
thought becomes word.*

44.

SYMBOLISM OF PURE AWARENESS

Mind deciphers the world in language of the symbolic. From forms, words, images, ideas, to people and things—everything is a symbol. Beyond the confines of the symbolic, lies pure awareness. Shiva is the symbol of this pure awareness from which the mind originates, and unto which the aspiring mind of a yogi dissolves. Shiva exists, either in reality or as a fragment of our imagination, and sure draws attention. He transfixes our gaze by his perfect physique, a magnetic persona with the moon as a head gear, fall of the Ganges from his locks, and his snake necklace. He is an emblem of benevolence and magnanimity, also called *bholenath*, the easily pleased one in a world of hard to please! His meditative posture exudes impeccable mastery of yoga, as well as defines the means of acquiring it. The snake wrapped around his neck is a symbol of tamed ego. Snow clad mountains in the backdrop symbolize an unagitated mind, seeped in the bliss of Self. His half smile connotes poise, and semi open eyes signify keeping a balance between spiritual and material realms. In the half moon adorned on Shiva's head, polarity meets. Dark and light forces balance out each other. His third eye represents an inner vision of reality. Worship Shiva, to go beyond the adventure of body-mind-intellect, and experience the ecstatic thrill of divine knowledge. Method of worshiping Shiva is simply remembering we are not apart from Shiva, and chanting *Shivoham!* Shiva I am!

To worship Shiva, you ought to become him.

45.

GODDESS WHO RIDES THE LION

Courage, like bank balance, must be built upon. Do not get comfortable with its first signs in your life! To strengthen your link with courage, invoke the goddess who rides the lion of desire. Worship Durga, who annihilates fear by her valor, ruthlessly destroys the enemy by her multitude of weapons, and adorns a garland of their skulls. A severed head in her one hand promises destruction of all that is evil, while a lotus in the other hand assures protection of the good. To invoke Durga, you need not revere her idol. Just visualize her magnificent form in front of your closed eyes. See her image expanding, growing vaster and bigger, enveloping and engulfing your small frame unto hers. Let her manifold hands and numerous weapons emerge from you, and her ferocious lion become your extension. Center yourself at the core of Durga. Become her. Hold this vision for a few minutes, till you experience an expansion, a growing sense of inner confidence. Replenished and fortified, gradually contract her image, and bring it to its original size, safely placing it in your heart. Now you are her embodiment, a divine force translating in action. You have the audacity to meet life with full force. You have the faculty to fight your battles, and win. You have become invincible, and possess the requisite boldness to destroy both desire and defeat.

When life demands courage, do not bargain your ferocity for surrender!

46.

BALANCE ENERGY BY AUM CHANT

There is a quiet corner in each of us where time does not exist, jolts of circumstance do not ruffle us; where death is a friend and life a game. We can access this corner at will, and remain stationed in it by the use of sound. After all, even a venomous snake can be tamed by sound, and so can the human monkey mind! As per *Rig Veda*—the oldest known Vedic Sanskrit text— *aum* is that primordial sound from which the cosmos emerged, and whose vibrations have the potency to merge us back in our source. It is nature's mantra, a symbol of pure consciousness. It is the subtlest of all idols, an antidote to energy imbalances, and a sound even the mute can produce. Letters of a-u-m represent the three states of consciousness—the waking, the dream and deep sleep. Reverberations of its chant transfix us in the fourth state of consciousness, the *turiya*, that is a state beyond all states. To derive the extraordinary benefits from this chant, utilize the sunrises and sunsets. That's when we are most receptive to absorbing its frequency. Assume a comfortable posture, breathe deeply to relax your mind, and let surface thoughts exhaust themselves. Now chant, keeping the measure of in-breaths and out-breaths proportional. Dwell on the interim gap between two chants. At the peak of concentration, the chant stops. There is no more sound of aum, no more thoughts, no more mind nor intellect. Cherish this most sacred moment. It is now when your individual soul has rubbed against infinity!

*We are the thirst of the Self
to experience itself.*

47.

SECRET OF SOHAM

One soul mate that stays with us all our life, literally from start to finish, is our breath. When it enters the body, we rejoice. When it leaves the body, we mourn. And in the middle, we forget all about it! Till the time it lives in us, it allows us to ponder on matters of religion and philosophy, and look for soul mates. When it departs, nothing remains to ponder about, and no one to ponder. Till the time breath gives us company, it lets us call ourselves so and so, and when it leaves, it lets others (who breathe) remember us as so and so. Breath is not just our sole connection to life, it is our one and only link to the place from where we came. The rhythm of our breath aches to tell us a great secret. Sound of inhalations proclaim *so* (That), and exhalations exclaim *ham* (I am). All our life, our breath begs to remind us *That I am,* while we keep thirsting for the relief of knowledge. The great revelation is muttered over and over with every rise and fall of our breath, while we keep ticking away like hands of a clock, building sand castles of wealth, fame and fortune. Breath is God, pleading to be noticed, heard, remembered. Listen intently to its plea, as you would to the rising and falling ocean waves, and you will begin to hear the sound of a million breaths, like little waves within the big wave. You will hear the stories of your many lifetimes, past gone and yet to come. Befriend the hissing notes of the great fire of breath. Heed the message of *soham*, the great liberation mantra.

Worship breath. It is God.

48.

BREATHE LIKE A TURTLE

A clever way to bridge the gap between helplessness and control, is acquiring conscious command of an unconscious process. Your breath. It is that life process, without which there is no life. Awareness and control of it results in gradual but sure mastery. Correct breathing awakens slumbering nerve channels, unlocks loftier states of consciousness, and can literally mean the difference between a czar and a slave! There is really no need to delve into intricate breath exercises. Simply observe your natural breathing, with the attitude of a witness. Just watch incoming and outgoing breath, and feel its warmth. Become aware of your lungs expanding and relaxing. Energy follows attention. By simply observing natural breathing, our breath grows long and deep. Now, direct your attention to the abdomen, observe the breath entering and exiting through the navel. This is the point where oxygen (traveling through mother's lungs, heart, uterus and placenta) first entered our body via the umbilical cord. Inhale through this very first gateway of breath, and infuse your cells and nerve channels with vitality. As you exhale, release all negativity and disease back through the belly. Watch the pause after inhalation, and after exhalation. These interludes are timeless moments, when you can sense an expansive emptiness. As you bring awareness back, resolve never to breathe in short quick gasps again, but taking your time!

Breath is the witness,
the recorder of our deeds.

49.

PRACTICE OF TREE MEDITATION

A seed tells the universe what it wants to become, and it is obeyed and served. Sounds marvelous, but it's a trap. We desire, and sooner or later, we create what we desire. Yet, the story does not end here. We crave yet again, and till such time all our longings see the light of day, we are enslaved to serve them through thought, word and deed. Desires are like the demon Raktabija, literal for 'blood-seed' who resurrected with each drop of his blood that fell on the ground, and was finally annihilated (freed) by Goddess Kali. To be freed from the captivity of desire, we need to destroy its seed. Saying this is the last, is a ploy that tricks us in the end. We need to simply exhaust what we have accumulated, and stop desiring further. We can also symbolically exhaust desires by practicing the tree meditation. Sit in a relaxed meditative posture. Imagine growing roots and getting firmly embedded to the ground. Slowly spread your branches to encircle the planet, becoming a wish-fulfilling tree with the ability to actualize all your wants. Meditate on one desire at a time. Visualize it forming bud, flowering and bearing fruit (coming to fruition). Feel the fullness, the satiety. Smile! Soon the pleasurable abundance reaches saturation, turning burdensome and heavy. It is time to let go. With graceful gratitude, allow the weight to drop. You have willed, manifested, experienced, and shed the mass of ambition. Now tread light on your feet, and direct all your attention to know the true purpose of your incarnation.

When desire drops, for and against dissolve.

50.

GO THE GOLDEN EGG WAY

In the beginning of creation, there was just a gigantic egg, floating about freely in the cosmos. The *Puranas* (sacred Sanskrit writings of Hindu legends and folklore) describe this as the golden womb that contained the worlds in embryonic form—the galaxies, planets, stars, winds, gods, demons and humans. It was the seat of pure potentiality, and countless creatures contained therein. Soon the egg grew in size, and creation took birth. Reason why another name of Brahma, the creator, is *hiranyagarbha* (golden womb). The womb is the origin of all life, and a symbol of unconditional nurturing of nature. There is a way to connect to this womb at will, and get recharged. Close your eyes, and visualize this humungous luminous womb of creation. Feel the profundity of what it is carrying. Now start directing a stream of its radiance to your heart, en route the crown chakra (six inches above your head). Let it blend in you, and emerge from your body to weave a luminous egg around you. Visualize yourself at its center, the yolk of this egg. Stay enveloped in this soft golden hue, till each cell of your body reflects its rays, and you beam like an elliptical glowworm emitting photons of light. Compulsion to find solutions from the outside will fade, as you smile with a silent certainty that you cause all that you create with the potency of Brahma. Yet, you are incessantly nursed by the universe like a babe.

You are the resplendent dream
of creation, born of a golden womb.

51.

SURYA YOGA—REFLECTING SUN'S LIGHT

Simple things get overlooked, that's the law of ordinary living. Paying attention to simple everyday occurrences, is the law of extraordinary living. We can count the number of wonderful episodes that get ignored everyday, to measure the extent of our ordinariness. But the complete forgetfulness of one of the most spectacular phenomenon on earth—the sun—makes our ordinariness gain some extraordinary proportions! We are able to call each day a day, only because of this event. Yet, most of us fail to acknowledge the fury, the grandeur and the resplendent descent of the rising light. Our entire life would get transformed if we were to simply bow to this favor of light that we are granted everyday without having to ask. We would inherit a fraction of its power. Every time we acknowledge something, even habitually, we internalize and begin to reflect a part of it. If you wish to radiate a fraction of sun's glow, start acknowledging it by doing sun salutations or offering water. By worshiping the sun, one worships trinity, as it is a manifestation of three distinct forms of energy. As it rises, it is the manifestation of Brahma, source of life. At noon, it contains the fiery aspect of Shiva. At dusk, it wears the calming vibration of Vishnu, the sustaining energy. Sun worship is the key to inner healing, longevity, acquisition of power, and wealth of both material and spiritual spheres. It lies at the core of *hatha* yoga.

*The void never speaks, but there
is always something to say to it!*

52.

THE EIGHT LIMBS OF YOGA

Yoga Sūtras of Patañjali elucidate how all life is either suffering or lack of suffering. Pain is hidden even in sources of pleasure, and there is no real joy to be found in material pursuits. Indeed, life is an everyday battle. It brings misery in various garbs, with occasional flashes of joy, and infrequent glimpses of the beyond. One moment we smile, the next moment we adorn a grimace. Bliss comes but in irregular doses. The real objective of yoga is stilling this patterning of consciousness, by realizing that the spring of lasting happiness is close, right within. The path of yoga lays down eight steps to arrive at this mindful awareness. These are *yama* (righteous living), *niyama* (disciplined obser-vances), *asana* (yoga postures), *pranayama* (breath work), *pratya-hara* (retracting the mind inwards), *dharana* (concentration), *dhyana* (meditation) and *samadhi* (absorption). These eight limbs of yoga are built like a pyramid, with each practice preparing us for the next. By disciplined practice, become the one who pulls the curtain and watches the show, rather than enacting forever on the stage of time. Throw life a challenge. Ask it to provoke your equilibrium, shatter your calm or pose you a riddle you cannot solve. Dare all those who sadden you to dishearten you this once. If you stand as your own obstruction to progress, defeat yourself by mastering those limitations that have always let you down. Learn to see serenity beneath turbulent waves of occurrence. Beneath the excitable senses, find the calm lake.

Do not practice equanimity.
See that equanimity exists.

53.

BRAHMANA—YOGA OF WANDERING

Did you know *brahmana* or wandering could be a form of yoga? Or rather, it can become one, if we alter the intent behind it. All that truly differentiates an act of yoga from an ordinary act is the intent. When we move in seeking, the steps that we take transform into a yogic act. This is the secret behind vagrancy of sages, ascetics and gypsies, who wander for different reasons, but at the base of their movement lies a burning quest. Thus, it is deemed a form of yoga. Nobody can truly wander without feeling uprooted from a common sense of belonging and comfort. Yet, nobody can wander for long without acquiring a unique sense of belonging and comfort, gained by sacrifice of the known. Arriving at this extraordinary state of rest by embracing unrest, is the reward of this penance. We too, can practice this yoga, and even without leaving our homes. Simply begin walking everyday, in seeking and in pain of an urgent enquiry, as though you would not stop till the doors are closed or until they open. Walk prayerfully, with intent, as though each step is unlocking your power, and unraveling the mystery. When you start walking every day at an assigned time, no matter where you are, things start moving in your life. Events begin to transpire faster. It is almost as though the burn rate of your karma increases, and your karmic load exhausts rapidly. Walk in solitude. Walk as though you will walk forever. Shed yourself in each step, become lighter in weight and swifter in spirit.

*Traveling is the only gauge of
how much load we are carrying.*

54.

CREATE YOUR OWN SOUL MATE

Did you know that your soul mate could be a rock, a tree or even rain? Yes, these seemingly inanimate objects are ideal for becoming a soul mate, because they are devoid of egoistic personalities. If you have trouble conceiving of a mate without a body of flesh, then perhaps you are not ready for a soul mate. To invite a soul mate into your life, you must transcend material conceptions, and sensitize yourself spiritually. Here's one method of converting a natural force into one. Begin with your favorite tree. Just pick the one you really like. Sit underneath it every day, around the same time, preferably during dawn or dusk, as communion is easier during these two times. Sit intuitively, let the tree's aura envelop you. Form a bond, share your story, and try listening to the tales of the tree. Embrace the trunk, and inhale the smell of the bark. Repeat this ritual for a week, and you would begin to feel comfortable in each other's presence. If you start to sense that the tree actually awaits your return, you have something going—a relationship on the spirit level. You will be amazed to see how well certain trees respond, how unconditional their love and giving is. They also offer protection and soul strength during tough times, and often prove more dependable than human company. The exchange is reciprocal, as your plain human touch is indeed precious to them as well. It makes them nostalgic, for they were once human, in a body of flesh, bone and blood, before they evolved into bodies of leaves, barks, and roots.

Be alone, to see what
continues to give you company.

55.

COLOR BATHS HEAL THE SOUL

How many times have you let yourself down, regretted words you never meant to say, or acted in ways you never intended? Oft the dark impelling surge of jealousy, greed and irrational fear overwhelm us so powerfully, that our reasoning mind is unable to exert an influence on our behavior. Where pious resolutions and will power fail, use of color works wonders, as it operates at a profound emotional plane. Practice taking color baths, and wash off layers of dirt accruing on the inside. Slow down your respiration, and place your palms on the knees facing up. Acknowledge your shortcomings. See them as a thick black oil in your spinal column, and make a strong intention to be freed from their hold. Now, visualize a liquid white light pouring over you, gradually pushing this black viscous oil down through your spinal column, through your feet, and into the earth, purging out the dark forces from your psyche. Next, perceive sunflower yellow on your crown for gaining clarity of thought, and bright red in the middle of your eyebrows for enhancing intuition. Picture peacock blue at the throat for acquiring self-control, and emerald green in your heart for gaining emotional clarity. With every inhalation, breathe in the color and hold it at each center for two to three minutes, while breathing normally. As you come under the influence of these benign hues, you can hope for a lasting change in your consciousness.

Being happy is itself a practice.
If you are not happy, pretend you are.

56.

MASTER THE MIND THROUGH THE BELLY

Our belly rages a constant fire, a fire that we call hunger. This fire constantly needs to be fed, from the moment of our conception till our dissolution. Feeding this fire is a sacred duty we perform quite regularly, mostly without awareness, and often without considering it sacred. How we feed this fire determines a lot of our destiny and happiness. Smart yogic practitioners know the link between the belly and the mind, and carefully choose their meals, besides the company they eat with. Moments of eating are moments of contemplation for them, as they watch the transformation of food into thought almost instantaneously. Whereas, for most of us, it is the contrary. Moments of eating are moments to get rid of our hunger in the fastest, and often most indulgent way. We continue to be swayed by forces of habit that make us gravitate towards unhealthy choices of foods and intoxicants. If we merely switch our mindset from eating to making an offering, a great shift occurs. Meal times become holy moments when we are being compassionate to ourselves, and worshipful to the divine fire. The quotient of purity in the food, and thereby our consciousness, increases manifold. When the food becomes purified, it becomes easier to still the modifications of the mind, and get attuned to the state we call yoga.

Stick to the sacred.

57.

EAT A POSITIVE PRANIC DIET

Purity of mind hinges on the purity of what we consume. Controlling food, one gets purified. Purified, one does not fault, and tendencies to go wrong are arrested. Really, we can't proceed far on our spiritual pilgrimage with a stuffy nose, digestive disorders, rapid pulse, perverted senses and short attention spans. Eating to please taste buds is foolish, since our alliance with food ends the instant it slides down our throats. It is the fire in the belly that actually eats. Let what you consume be a sacrificial offering to this fire, and offer only those foods that do not produce a foul smell when sacrificed. This is a simple litmus of what is life promoting (positive *prana*), and what is life negating (negative *prana*). Every time we ingest fried or overcooked food, dead meat and intoxicants, we increase physical toxicity, psychic inertia, and compromise our inner harmony. Switch from negative foods that take away from your energy repertoire, to a positive *pranic* diet that adds to it. Consume nature's fresh produce, that heals and satiates like mother's milk. Quit using food as a source of entertainment, gluttony or blood shed, and get equipped with calm nerves, pure bloodstream and a mind sensitized to subtler realms. Ultimately, this path of discriminatory eating leads to a total disregard for the body itself. As Shankaracharya elucidates in *Vivekachudamani*, harboring attachment to the body while aspiring for salvation, is like holding onto a crocodile while crossing the river.

Right eating is the shortest distance between hunger and satiety.

58.

SPIRITUALITY OF HEALING

Ayurveda is an ancient body of knowledge attributed to Dhanvantari, the physician to the gods in Hindu mythology. Contained in the sacred Sanskrit texts of *Atharva Veda*, it was originally shared as an oral tradition. It has begun to be commonly understood as a set of healing medicines and massages. What is not commonly understood, however, is how this healing occurs. Ayurveda aims to understand the five elements, or the five sheaths of which human life is comprised. Its systematic healing is also comprised of five methodologies called *panch-karma*, that lead to inner purification. Ayurveda is much more. It is a retreat back to our original nature. It is an acknowledgement of the incompleteness of modern medical science, and a reminder to address the soul presiding in the physical body. It proposes that true healing becomes possible when we close existential gaps. The question before any spiritual practitioner is where and whence do these gaps arise, and how do imbalances occur. On physical and mental planes, the restoration is achieved by correcting and redirecting the life force inside the body. On a spiritual plane, the wholeness is restored by cleansing and rinsing karmic sheaths, such that layers and layers of karmic impression are eradicated from the root, and do not recur. In actuality, if you are serious about understanding the science of Ayurveda, you will be led back to the quintessential question Ramana Maharishi asked—who am I?

Receive with gratitude.
Relinquish with grace.

59.

YOGIC USES OF SLEEP

Yoga describes sleep state as a necessary part of the soul's journey back home. During sleep, we return to our original state that was interrupted upon acquiring a physical body. *Samadhi* is similar to sleep but with a difference. In sleep, the consciousness is present but not alert. It is hidden, like the tree in a seed. In samadhi, the seed is cracked, and consciousness is alert. Sleep can become samadhi by joining sleep with awareness, and we can utilize our nights for higher workings. The question is how to stay awake in sleep, when it is difficult to be alert even during the day! Sleep consciousness can be effectively utilized only after the waking mind has made some progress. In other words, once we can stay aware during wakeful state, this awareness can be carried into sleep state. One way to fall asleep with alertness, is to assume *chinmudra* (gesture of consciousness), and maintaining this throughout sleep. It is assumed by joining tip of the thumb and index finger, while slightly extending the remaining three fingers. When dream waves throw you in different directions, awareness on this mudra brings you back to awareness. With continued practice, you will glimpse a state of alert sleep, when you will be 'enough awake' in your sleep to know that you are dreaming. This knowledge, when translated back to waking state, will allow you to know that life is a dream posing real. Now your sleep would have turned into your most precious practice.

Nothing is worse than losing integrity to a dream.

60.

HARNESSING DREAM POWER

Dreams can play the role of a spiritual teacher in our life, if treated as such. When faced with an irresolvable dilemma, dream guidance is worth more than hours of rational brainstorming. Each time we sleep, we can expect to receive symbolic cues, past life insights, health warnings, miraculous healing and glimpses of our calling. So next time you sleep, try to be fully awake! This is when our conscious mind block is set aside, and we are receptive to higher realms. To harness dream power, make a mental request for guidance just before falling asleep, in the semi-conscious state between waking and sleeping. Pose your query concisely. Sleep reclining on your back, such that your head is slightly raised facing up, never to the sides. Keep your neck in a straight line, not bent. Keep your palms facing down, parallel to the sides of your navel. Keep your feet parallel. Alternatively, interlock the palms and place over the navel, and loosely interlock your feet, not the legs. Listen to the sound of your breath, feel its warmth. Stay in this meditative posture in an attempt to simply rest, not sleep. Be attentive to flashes of intuition, images or sounds you may see or hear, as these may be in response to your request. Later or next day, jot down all that you recall, even if doesn't appear to be much. Honing a connection with your dream life takes time and devotion, just like with any partnership. When you get attuned to your dream directives, your steps gain spiritual momentum.

Let your heart pace with a frantic obligation to end all dreaming.

61.

DREAM TO MUKTI CONSCIOUSNESS

What appears is not true. Or rather it is as true as the fanciful imagination of a drugged person. What is seen is not fixed, or it is as fixed in reality as a reflection trembling on water; its pattern as coincidental as the pattern of color splashed on canvas. The physical reality that meets our perception is as transient as the apparatus with which it is perceived—the physical eye. When you perceive reality to be relative, you get aligned with a different perception, the one that frees you in multiple ways. The distinction between spirit and matter dissolves, and you see life for it really is, a hallucination. The tight grasp of seeming reality loosens, and you begin to walk on a path that contains a hope of unraveling who you truly could be. To feel like an element of a dream, like a wish afloat in a heart or like a blob of nature's reverie is a unique experience. Practice this perception. Bring the dreamlike fluidity into your real life, and stop seeing situations as blocks of concrete events, seemingly defying much change. Rather view them as pliable, dynamic and unreal. Only in ascribing permanence to impermanence, do we suffer. While perceiving anything with your physical eye, remind yourself that it is a dream, feel the bluff. The recognition of this dream consciousness itself is *mukti* or freedom consciousness. In its wake, you invariably become the witness, the dreamer who just stirred awake.

Let there be two selves.
One who feels; other that witnesses.

62.

SHED CLOTHES OF CONDITIONING

Clothes are intimately related to the roles we play in life. They mirror who we are, and remind us who we are. Often they go beyond that, and dictate who we are as well. They also circumscribe who we can be. First they remind us of our identity, and then keep us confined to it. They monitor the play. On a subtler level, clothes symbolize conditioning. We wear clothes of our conditioning, and hide behind layers of acquired learning, concealing and revealing our various selves under different contexts. If you wish to change your life script, change your attire. Your self-perception and response would alter automatically. It is an important tool you should not feel hesitant to use. Drop the force of habit, shed your old way of dressing like snakes shed their skin. Get uncomfortable. Play with identities. When a monk wears one color—ochre, he is communicating his synthesized and singular pursuit in life, which is working towards salvation. There is no conflict or confusion in his personality, not even multifaceted-ness. His life has condensed to one burning quest, and that reflects in his clothing. There is something sacred about holding onto one color, one thought, one goal, in exclusion to everything else. This focused attention converges our energy to a powerful zone of creativity, and contains the secret to accumulating personal power.

You have got one life to be mad.
Don't waste it in pursuit of sanity.

63.

MAKE NIGHT TIME YOUR CONFIDANTE

We know opposites attract. Darkness in this regard, is the perfect match for our soul's brilliance. Armed with darkness, we get equipped to enter our own light. As worldly attractions and distractions get engulfed by its black stillness, we are directed to look within. Night time represents the womb, from whence we emerge, and unto which we dissolve. Each night we commune with it, and emerge rested and refreshed to meet another day. It is the real confidante of our soul. Who else can be, other than the one that gives birth, creates and finally devours us. It is important to bond with this womb consciously, in order to strengthen our connection with our source. Here is one way to do it. Simply sit in pitch dark for a while before you fall asleep. Stare into the darkness spread around you, hear its stillness. In this setting, recall the events of the day as though you are watching a movie. You may recall missed details, or overlooked conversations, but continue to review them objectively as an observer. The real event is the burning, the consummation, your melting away into the ink. Hold this moment dearly, as you are entering a territory of pure potentiality, irrationality and instinct. Drop all defenses, and offer yourself fully to the night, like a child returning to mother's lap. As your melt inside the dark womb, feel the inner light burn brighter. Now hidden doors slam open, and the dialogue ensues between you and yourself.

Work on accepting yourself,
than changing yourself.

64.

SECRET OF INNER SPEECH

You sometimes have to prove yourself all over again, to your own self! One effective way to counter self-doubt is to change your inner speech. Let us admit, during most of our waking hours we are thinking, and this thinking involves a great deal of language or talking to oneself. The idea is to change this self-talk to a positive one. When you chat with yourself, say sweet words. Uncover the damaging verbiage that you often repeat under your breath, without ever quite realizing it. Expose your (often irrational) statements by stating them loud and clear, and replace them with more realistic, and less punishing ones. Switch from 'I do it all wrong' to 'I can actually do it right' and from 'I messed it up' to 'I am improving.' Make sure that you replace discouraging talk with measured and believable optimism, and enforce it with repetition. Plant inspirations in place of accusations. Reserve notes of praise, encouragement and courage for your inner ears. We know that words have tremendous power. One letter here and there is the difference between an argument, and an agreement. The moment you reverse your inner dialogue, your emotions begin to turn. Load of negativity in your bloodstream dilutes, and your dying faith in yourself revives. It's not a surprise, that a mere mental repetition of positive speech, initially even without true conviction, brings about sea change. Now, if a nagging voice is telling you it can't be that simple, challenge it!

Mind what you speak,
even in sleep. It leaves a trace.

65.

COLLECTING WORD POWER

There is an extremely simple way to collect power, and that is to say what you mean, and do what you say. Words have power, because they are the physical manifestations of intent. They have sound, they have wave form, and they have intent. Therefore uttered words are alive, as much as we are! They not only symbolize who we are, they often decide who we become. Every time we open our mouth to speak, we have a choice. Like any other power, word power can diminish through frivolous and reckless use. When we utter words we do not mean, give words we do not keep, or downright distort the truth, we lower the scale of personal power. Consistently keeping our word programs the universe to pair our words with truth, and whatever we utter begins to manifest. Speaking is like creating an image. To create a beautiful vocal image, silence yourself before you speak. Then, what would emerge would be pure, and you would have perfected one important posture of yoga—*vac siddhi* or the power of creation with sound. It does *not* result from activating the throat chakra, rather once you attain this power, the throat chakra (quite naturally) gets activated. Himalayan saints of yore were masters of this yoga. The syllables they uttered in meditative states became mantras, empowered sacred sounds, that give us access to a whole different power—God's power.

Words are alive. If you cut one, it will bleed.

66.

GIVE YOUR HEART AN EAR

There is perpetually a soft whisper tugging at our heart, telling us what to do. An inner voice overlooks and comments on everything that happens to us, and through us. This gentle (almost inaudible) utterance is our inner guide. If we heed its tutelage, all problems will get solved. In fact, they will not arise. Often this guidance that springs from our very core, and forever within our reach, gets lost in the chatter of our logical mind. The neglect of this mumble costs us dearly, sometimes our entire life. We move far away from where we were meant to be. For right action to flow spontaneously and effortlessly, befriend this voice. Give it ear. Forget reason. Move solely by the dictates of your heart. During moments of conflict or confusion, take a deep breath, put forth the query to your heart and wait. Or mentally place your choices in each palm, and create a bridge of light from your heart into your palms. When the response comes (expect it to be instantaneous), it will be in the form of a tingling or heaviness in one of your palms. Notice how your body reacts to the choice placed in this palm, and the sense it emanates. If it is one of comfort and ease, you have received the answer. The reply may not always be what you wish to hear, but will surely be for your highest good. When both choices seem to respond to the query, the apparent conflict may be an illusion.

*What you seek, has been
waiting for you all along.*

67.

YOGA OF NON-DISCIPLINE

Practice of discipline is crucial to control the wavering mind. When we are aligned with discipline, we are aligned with grace. Yet, beware of bondage in all guises, especially the guise of discipline. We form stringent routines and end up getting so attached to them, that they extract more than give. Controlled by habit and every day rituals, like sipping coffee from the same mug, or meditating at the same spot everyday, is not going to take us far for very long. Familiarity makes us habituated to seeing things a certain way, and overlook the newness that each day brings. All were good if life did not spring on us strange surprises, or corner us in situations not always congenial to comfort. Yoga of non-discipline keeps us alert and nimble for whatsoever life may present. It is simple. Whenever a sensory experience becomes habitual, it is time to stop that practice. Do not always suit yourself. Break your routine every once in a while, sleep on a different bed or in another room. Make yourself uncomfortable. Switch your diet. If you are boastful about punctuality, delay yourself one day. If you are a perfectionist, make one deliberate mistake. Discipline and indiscipline yourself at will, always remaining the one who decides. The idea is to be finally free of both. Remember, the yoga of non-discipline will only bear fruit when you know what discipline is all about. Only masters unchain their pets!

Avoid familiarity—it makes us miss.

68.

LOVE AND COOK WITH ABANDON

Love and cook with abandon, says Rumi, the great Sufi mystic and poet. True for anything that we do, but more so for loving and cooking! These are two actions that give us sustenance, nourishment, and escape velocity into other dimensions. Both, if tended carefully and consistently, give the sweetest reward, and if rendered with even a wee bit of restraint, completely fail to give delight. Giving ourselves totally to the act of cooking, gives us insights into how to love fully. When you love or cook, make the process itself the goal, and steer clear from purpose. Let no expectation, fear of failure or need for appreciation mar the flow. Expectation confines what we can create, and fear gives us restraint where there should be none. One can derive an unimaginable measure of joy from heating the oil, slicing and dicing vegetables, simmering broth, monitoring temperatures, playing with spices, and watching flavors mesh. Cooking with mindful awareness adds an invisible new flavor to our meals, and gives us vitality of a different kind. Loving with abandon teaches many important lessons about life's transforming power. We experience the bliss of being in the present moment, and can extend this practice to everything that we do in each wakeful hour.

If you know love, there is little
need to know anything else.

69.

NURTURE PLANTS TO GET HEALED

Being near nature is healing, tending to nature is even more so. When we nurture plants, we symbolically give to them the love we could never give to ourselves. When we water them, we nurse our souls. As we trim them regularly, and make sure they don't turn unruly, we become tidier in our personal lives. We also learn how not to allow negative tendencies to outgrow our good intent. In situations of acute anxiety or stress, take up the responsibility of nurturing a few plants. Even if you weep as you water them, your grief will dry off, and a smile shall return to your lips most miraculously. Form a relationship with plants, and feel the joy of their simple unconditional existence. Offer them the right environment for growth. Supply them with nutrients, and right portion of water, shade and sunlight. Learn about them, know their botanical names, and investigate their unique characteristics and benefits. Notice how they grow into what they contain in seed, just like us, and how their dormant potential flourishes with nurturing. Observe how noiselessly they branch out, fruit, flower and fall, without making a hue and cry over every little happening. Touch the flowers with reverence for the journey they traversed, and for what they have accomplished. When you gaze at them with love, they seem to return your exchange. Rinse the leaves frequently, just as we need to constantly rinse and renew our spirit.

When you love, you become infinitely capable of everything.

70.

YOGA OF HARDSHIPS

"Know that sorrow, being the means of convincing man of the need of inner life, is a spiritual teacher," says *The Rosary of Gems*, a Tibetan text. Undoubtedly, those who have suffered listen sooner to a spiritual message. This is not to glorify suffering, but to drive home the fact that how we handle distress reflects (and determines) our spiritual progress. The yoga of hardships is something we simply put into play as soon as we spot anguish creeping into our life. As soon as times begin to get tough, tighten your guards and be attentive. Instead of getting swept away in grief, go to the source of this fountain. Practice *sakshi bhava*, the attitude of a witness, and find out who feels the pain. Only through observation can you destroy afflictions, advises Patanjali, the father of yoga *sutras*. The entire range of yogic exercises, including physical postures, breath control, meditations and concentration are designed to inculcate the witness consciousness. Another fallout of suffering is that it intrinsically lessens our karmic load by exhausting negative karma. These are indeed times to pay back for something that we may not remember, but nature's records do. These are times to study our suffering, and ascertain its cause within ourself. When we have the humility to take responsibility for our pain, and acknowledge our hardships to be self-earned, we become qualified to receive subtler insights.

The only way to be free of a situation,
is to be free in it.

71.

FORGIVENESS IS PENANCE

It is the curtain of the mundane that keeps us from realizing how special life really is. It makes us take life for granted, often hurting the very people we love, or holding grudges. In the few years that you walk with life, and illumine this body, let magnanimity walk with you. Realize that only giving can enrich, and giving up can set you free. Forego the unnecessary burden of guilt and grudges. Close your eyes, your windows to the world, and visualize five people who may have caused you hurt. As you breathe in, acknowledge the hurt accumulated inside of you. Locate where it is hiding in your body, and bring it to your belly. Now, breathing out, expunge it decisively by mentally saying, 'I forgive you heartily as God forgives me, for my highest good, and for the highest good of the universe. So be it.' Personalize, and repeat this exercise as long as needed. Now recall five individuals you have hurt. Repeat this little prayer, asking forgiveness for yourself, and *from* yourself. After all, hurt is the same, and what you have given out resides in you equally. Asking for forgiveness and forgiving in this manner is more potent than asking it directly. You are contacting individuals (and yourself) at a soul level by use of breath, and bypassing the resistance of the mind. Also, forgiveness is an act of penance, that has more to do with you than the other. When saints and priests ask you to forgive, they are simply showing you a way to transform yourself.

When you have nothing left to give,
give one more time.

72.

SEARCH YOUR CHILDHOOD FOR CUES

One way to reach our source, the pure potentiality from where we have emerged, is to retrace our step and move backward in time. Go back year by year, to the last five years, the last ten, and slowly reach your childhood. Recall your perception of the world, and of yourself at the time. Allow minute details of your childhood events, people, sights and smells to spring up from your psyche. You will be amazed to know how intimately you are still linked to your childhood years. What you were most inclined to do then, is often the pointer to your present life choices, and conflicts. Recognizing your sibling rivalries, rebellion, tantrums or seemingly innocent childish cruelties, contain the key to remedy mental blockages, and even physical ailments. Just staring at your past with wide open eyes, and looking at facts without judgement or prejudice, releases you of them. When similar situations now arise, your reactions would have changed. Go back still further by connected breathing, i.e., breathing steadily with no pauses between filling and emptying your lungs. This will help stimulate regression to the first event of your life, your birth experience. Stop here. Ask yourself, 'where did I come from, what caused this body that I inhabit' and 'where was I before this?' This is a powerful line of questioning wherein lies the clue to life's most baffling mystery. Find out, what was that one desire that put you at the mercy and whim of the dark womb, and suffer the turmoil of birth. If at this moment you are able to travel still further in time, you may dip your feet in that ocean for which mortals thirst.

Recognition itself is resolution.

73.

FAST—TO REACH THE DIVINE FAST

Fasting is a human resolve to surmount all that is human. Fasting is a rebellion against habitual urges that are bent on keeping us captive. It's an effort to access subtler realms, while encased in flesh. It is a means to find joy that must sleep in this mundanity. Days of fasting are special days, when the body and mind slowly subjugate to our will, defeated in their effort to break our resolve, and the spirit rises to bow to its source. So starve your belly and your mind of unnecessary fodder every once a while, in the name of God! Tame your sense horses to lose their potency by fasting for three, seven, eleven, twenty one or forty days every quarter. These are holy numbers with powerful occult symbolism of their own, that lend strength to your penance. Improvise your own bans. Restrict your diet to fruit and vegetables, one meal a day after sunset, or a zero carb diet. Just anything will do for a start. Supplement fasting with a stipulated number of mantra chanting, that you can complete each day with ease. Do not over commit and under perform. Over some days of following this discipline, something other than you compels you to rise above yourself. Your lips start to reject strong taste, your mind drops the weight of heavy unrefined thoughts, and a hunger for the divine holds sway. Note, that the manner of breaking your vow is as crucial as observing it. As the time of the meal approaches, do not rush in the direction of tinkling plates. Rather, proceed with the restraint and dignity of one who could wait more.

Let life live you. Become the channel.

74.

ELIMINATE EXCESS TO BE IN YOGA

There is power in saying *no* to what you do not need in your life. Indeed, we need very little, and accumulating the unnecessary is a huge contributor to our nameless existential strife. Eliminating excess is indeed a great spiritual endeavor, and a sure stride towards a yogic lifestyle, because excess is the antithesis of yoga. Being masters of excess, we cannot hope to become masters of yoga, which is the path of renunciation. Look around you, and you will spot many a thing, many a habit, many an association, and many an obligation you can do without. Most of our obligations are self imposed, and merely fan the ego by giving a false sense of purpose. They really do not exist. If you are serious about following the path of yoga, know that you have one obligation alone, and that is to figure out who you are, and why you are here. If you are serious about yoga, know that yoga is about giving up. It is not about acquiring. Start by eliminating clothes from your wardrobe you haven't worn for years, and eating not a bite more than your hunger dictates. Ponder on what you can eliminate next, such as unsupportive friendships, habits, or web of plans and ambitions that crowd your mind. You will feel lighter in spirit from doing this simple exercise, besides conserve energy, the subtle part of you. The luster in eyes of mystics is this accumulated energy that they have cherished, and chiseled. So can you.

Possess less and less. Become more and more.

75.

PRAY AND TILT THE ENERGY SCALE

In nature, everything is weighed and measured. There are no boons granted by gods. It's physics, the science of matter and energy, the law of how things work. Prayer also operates in the field of our goals (matter) and energy (intent), and their interaction determines the outcome. Prayer is nothing but wanting something sufficiently enough, to tilt the scales of destiny in our favor. Reason why things may not work the way we want them, is we did not want them enough! There is absolutely nothing that you can't get if you want it bad enough, *and* for the right reasons. These are the only two conditions to be met for the apple to fall right in your lap with least effort. As Paramhansa Yogananda says, always desire that which is good, noble and pure. Then, as a divine force, filled with the magnetism of God, you can never fail to attract anything you want. Prayer is merely an act of solidifying our motive, converging divergent thoughts, and rinsing our conscience, so that rays of our intent are shining bright and clear. What we are actually doing when we are praying, is clearing the air, dispelling pollutants, and focusing energy in one direction. Any impurities existing in our body-mind apparatus that may block our desires from blossoming, are eradicated through prayer.

*Return is not possible for a
benediction that has been granted.*

76.

UNDERSTAND THE LAWS OF KARMA

Lightly touch a blade of grass, and it trembles forever. Estimate how many chords we have struck till now, and how long the music shall continue to roll. This echo of our actions, the gradual inevitable momentum of our deeds, is what is termed fate or karma. Karma is born, when from an embodied being, objects fall off but not the relish for them! When desire is born again and again, we are caught in karma. When we leave jobs half done (akin to half shaven heads in a barber shop), we continue to be reborn. Till we view life in two shades of black and white, we are gripped by duality, and enmeshed in karma. Understand the inevitability, that as parts of one indivisible whole, when we hurt another, sooner or later we feel the burn. There are no other records kept, nor is the vengeance of an unseen authority unleashing on us. Karma is personal luggage, that can neither be shared nor wished away, only exhausted. To break its spell and go beyond its confines, be complete in every act. Take each act to perfection, whether it is walking, eating, working or resting. Fully absorb the lessons imparted by life at each stage, and do not utter promises that you fail to keep. Or else all these shall hunt you down, seeking completion. Why? Because you initiated them! Most importantly, stop reacting partially to circumstance. Be even in adversity and fortune, and become an equal stranger to rebuke and praise. Understand, that till you assert a personality, with its idiosyncrasies and preferences, life will continue to craft your unique character in its script.

Body is the residue of our karma.

77.

PLAN YOUR NEXT INCARNATION

It is with a sense of urgency that we must plan our next incarnation, because it is fanciful to imagine this birth to be your last, unless you have evidence to suggest otherwise! Till the time desire exists, we keep getting incarnated into different forms. Thus, unless you can claim to be free of desire, intelligently game planning your next birth, supporting circumstances and environment is critical to our growth. Considering the impermanence and unpredictability that marks life on earth, any moment could be our last. We cannot afford to have a vague undefined last thought in this body. Till the time we breathe, we can influence the decision of our next incarnation to some extent, by consciously visualizing and intending our next address. Towards this end, we must formulate our forthcoming incarnation that would most suitably fulfill our leftover desires, and keep this vision firmly embedded in our minds at all times. Just as our last thought before falling asleep is carried forward to the next day upon waking up, the last thought of our life is carried forward to our next birth. Your idea of where you want to be and what you wish to manifest, must be crystal clear in your head at all times. Such that when the moment of death arrives, it is not feared, rather welcomed as the carrier to your desired destination.

Human birth is a tunnel we
need pass through to see light.

78.

SUFI WAY OF REFLECTION

If you take a peek at your routine, you may find yourself ticking about like a clock, performing barren duties. Or surrounded by things you do not need, and indulging in rituals that do not satisfy your soul. You may sense that something terribly important is missing. If you think further and carefully, you may discover with dismay that in your apparently fulfilling life, what you truly thirst for is absent. Like quietude, joy and contentment. Or a few moments to hear the twitter of birds, and ponder where you are headed. When life begins to defy meaning, try the Sufi way of reflection. Just before retiring to sleep each night, take account of all that you have done during the day. Examine your different states of mind, and correlating actions. Reflect on which pursuits were really worth struggling for, and which were merely sapping time and resources. Find out what has been achieved through striving, and what has been granted through grace. Question what is your true need. Align yourself to your soul's purpose, and let your actions be in response to a higher inspiration, rather than personal motives. Eliminate more and more of those actions in which greed is involved, and render service selflessly. Discipline yourself through sheer will, and guard your awareness as a dog watches over its master. As you go about the business of living with such discrimination, the same clockwise routine will steer you to freedom.

World of the mundane induces sleep.
Call of the mystic awakens.

79.

ABSTAIN—IT'S EASY!

One of the eight limbs of *ashtanga* yoga is *yama* or abstinence. Abstinence may appear like a difficult practice, but it is simple. Once you value how precious you really are, you will naturally and willfully abstain from anything that tarnishes that purity. If intellectual discrimination to choose the right path appears hard to follow, just fall in love with your inner beauty, and sacredness. Then, abstinence from untruth, violence, covetousness, and indulgences will come easy. You will naturally begin to guard the treasure that you are, and assume the posture of restraint. We have the blessing of voluntary movement, and can assume any posture at our will—posture of love, posture of dance, posture of inspiration. True practice of yoga is not just about assuming physical postures. Rather, it is about perfecting mental postures that surmount greed, indulgences, apathy, lethargy, doubt, and delusion. With each little gesture, a string of gestures is formed, and with a string of gestures a lifetime is formed. Yoga is the science of refining our everyday mental postures. All we have to do is change their angle a wee-bit, manipulate the sequence a bit, and we could arrive at a far greater harmony than we ever imagined. We are in yoga (union) with our source at all times. We are already there! The whole journey is an act of realizing it.

*Material pursuits and
spiritual quest cannot cohabitate.*

80.

THE FINAL POSTURE

Life is short, shorter are moments instilled with the awareness that it is so. Time is fleeting. With each passing hour, we near death. With each passing year, we watch our loved ones disappear like formation of clouds. The final posture we assume in this life is the posture of death, when we physically lie cold as stone. Any moment the hour that brings death may come. Reincarnation is a reassuring concept that affirms our continuity, but let it not turn us complacent or recklessly procrastinate the task at hand. We must rise in this life, not in the next. The final posture of *hatha* yoga is also *shavasana* or the corpse pose, for good reason. *Shava* literally means a dead body in Sanskrit, and the corpse pose is a reminder of the end while the journey is on. It begs us to remember the transience of life, so we may live with greater awareness. After engaging in strenuous postures, the yoga session is concluded by laying on the back, with half-closed eyes, feet separated, and palms facing upwards. The body is held loosely without a trace of strain, and viewed as though a lifeless corpse is spread out on the floor. Complete physical relaxation is achieved through this posture, but its hidden symbolism must be meditated upon while assuming it. After laying in this asana when we rise, we must rise a new person, one who has consciously tasted the rest and rejuvenation of death. Let this final posture of yoga propel us to reflect upon our mission for this lifetime, and move single-mindedly towards accomplishing it.

Death is a kiss of the beloved—
it changes you forever.